The Poetry of Chantay Mahogany's Life.....and Yours!

Chantay Mahogany

Kria,

I hope really enjoy this book.

Chantay Mahogany

Bloomington, IN

authorHOUSE

Milton Keynes, UK

AuthorHouse™
1663 Liberty Drive, Suite 200
Bloomington, IN 47403
www.authorhouse.com
Phone: 1-800-839-8640

AuthorHouse™ UK Ltd.
500 Avebury Boulevard
Central Milton Keynes, MK9 2BE
www.authorhouse.co.uk
Phone: 08001974150

First published by AuthorHouse 5/10/2006

ISBN: 1-4259-0564-1 (sc)

Printed in the United States of America
Bloomington, Indiana

This book is printed on acid-free paper.

Photographer: David York

Dedication

In loving memory of my grandmother, Connie Mae Hart, whose childhood conversations of encouragement and affirmation never left my heart.

I love you Grandma!

Introduction

A good deal of my life's journey has been spent in looking for the good in people. Most of the time I've found it hiding under many layers of "stuff" – hurt, fear, anger and low self-esteem.

While traveling down that same road of disappointment, failure and self-deception, I learned how to go around the pot holes and the "greener grass." Each time I hit a bump in the road, I became stronger (but only after I stopped feeling sorry for myself) and found the courage to make the choice to change direction and move forward.

My heartfelt desire for you is that the footprints on these pages will encourage you to stay the course of your journey, to keep your eyes on the road, to watch out for the lesson signposts and to learn to make good choices for change.

You CAN Make It!

Table of Contents

Love...

Religion...

Children...

As a child, I watched each of us being treated differently.
Favoritism and manipulation created confusion,
pain and self-doubt in us all.
Later, division and isolation set in, and our
lives became a series of bad choices
that led us down different and destructive paths
until we weren't even friends anymore.
Good parenting is a choice to treat everyone
equally with love and respect.

How are you choosing?

An Education
on Creating a Child!

I'm talking to you -- young woman!
Before you lay down and have sex
and create a child – **THINK!**
That young man and you just want to feel good
and express to each other what you feel is love, but,
without commitment, it's really just lust.
Well, young lady, when you decide to
"back that thang up" I hope you realize you're backing your entire
life up! I know you think you're grown up. He tells you all the
nice things you want to hear. Unfortunately, the **real education**
comes after the babies are born, and as a young mother,
you have to learn how to be a mother,
while you try to teach your child.
This makes life very hard.
That young man will walk away 75% of the time
because he has his entire life in front of him,
and he didn't really want a child –
he just wanted to have a good time.
So young mother, you're left on your own
for your family and the government to help you.
Why not get **your education** on life and responsibility
BEFORE having sex.

Get Your Education First!

Character and Children

It is very important that we teach our children character.
It is not enough to house them, clothe and feed them.
There are many more tasks at hand
when we take on the job of raising a child.

Character issues arise very early in childhood.
If you have more than one child,
never show favoritism over the other children.
This can and will be very damaging to the other siblings.
You also harm the favored child as well.
This child takes on a false sense of pride
and a nobility that is not true.

Teach the children togetherness
and the importance of family unity.
Favoritism creates division among children
and sows the seeds of anger and resentment in them.
When combined, these things tear down the family structure
and create poor character in our children.

We must teach our children to share with others
and show them how not to be selfish and self-centered.

Remember – the kind of child you raise
will become the same kind of adult.

Teach Character!

Raising Our Children

It is our extreme duty to raise our children
with a firm and loving perspective.
It is not a job that we negotiate with them about.
We should teach the children lessons on responsibility
so they will be on the path of becoming
reasonable and intelligent young adults.

Friendship is not a key factor in raising our children.
Teaching them discipline and character
is what is important.
In most cases they will be angry with you
about the lessons you are giving them;
but in the long run they will thank you
for staying the course with them.

Be a Parent First and a Friend Second!

Family...

Even though we're all related, we are still very different people.
We need to see that love, acceptance and encouragement of diversity
in each other are what give us the sense of belonging
that makes a family good...and strong!

How's your eyesight?

The Family

The old days, when wood had to be chopped,
cotton had to be picked; the vegetables were planted;
the family stood together.
Communities stood as one; what happened?
We have more and yet we have less.
We have less compassion and love for each other.
I know we all must live our lives the best that we can.
We are separated by more than the miles we live apart.
We don't choose our family.
This is given by the sovereign and loving hand of God.
I see families separated by cars, houses, jobs, titles,
money and discrimination.
I see old grudges and long-standing family feuds
getting the best of people.
The funeral is the largest gathering of the family
besides the family reunion.
We can change this if we want to.
The power lies in each and every one of our hearts.
Peace and Blessings to All the Families.

A Daughter's Prayer

I pray, mother, that you will not choose a favorite child
among us, but love us all equally.
Some children are stronger and some are weaker.
I pray that you will give the weak one an extra boost,
but love us all the same.
Showing favoritism hurts the other children.
Most of all, it really hurts the favored one in the long run.
I pray that you will teach us
togetherness, love and sharing – but most of all,
how to be kind to each other.
I pray that you will lead by example
and not just tell us to do as you say and not as you do,
because this program does not work.
I pray that you will be a woman full of wisdom
and not foolishness.
I pray, mother, that you will teach us the truth
about how to live in the real world – with fewer surprises,
so we will be better prepared to face life
with wisdom and courage.

This is my prayer!

A Sister's Prayer

I pray that you, my sister, will not try to use me or
manipulate me for your own benefit.
I pray that you will not lie to me or about me.
We may not always agree on all situations,
but I pray that we can agree to disagree
and have regard for one another.
It is wrong to personally attack and hurt each other.
This act not only harms us as sisters,
but also harms the entire family.
Yes, we are sisters, but we are very different people,
living life in very different ways.
I can respect that, and I hope you can, too.

This is my prayer!

You Are Still My Father

Even though you live somewhere else
with that other lady and her kids,
You are still my father.
You are there playing house with
another man's family that he ran out on.
I have never understood the concept of one man raising
another man's children when he has children of his own.
Even though you chose to run away from
your responsibilities as a father and a man,
You are still my father.
Just because you and my mother realize that
there's nothing more between the two of you except me,
that does not relinquish you of your parental duties.
Coming around on my birthday and Christmas
does not make you a good father. Buying me the latest
pair of Jordans isn't what parenting is all about!
You are still my father.
Many men are hiding within the walls of other families
trying to forget about their real responsibilities –
the ones they created and walked away from.

You Are Still My Father!

Friends...

The Lord brings people into our lives for a
purpose. All are not meant to stay.
They teach us how to have the courage to keep
the healthy, constructive relationships
and how to walk away from the unhealthy, destructive ones.

Who are you keeping?

Distant Friend

I see you from afar, we gaze at each other and give noncommittal smiles. That's all I get in the company of others. I realize you have built a thick wall around yourself. I see you again, alone this time--your smile runs deep inside of me. I feel your need, but I'm very reluctant to address it. I feel your pain which you deliver through your words and the way you live your life. I believe I know what the root of the problem is; I desperately want to reach out to you. Friend you are so far away even when sitting in the same room; your thoughts leave without permission. I want to be your friend; I feel like I've known you for sometime now. I have read you cover to cover and stumbled upon some painful chapters. The chapters are very familiar, and I wonder how you deal with your pain. I guess you think its best to keep everything in and everyone out. I see you friend; we are a lot alike in our differences. One day I will tell you what a wonderful person you are, should you ever allow yourself to bloom. I want you to reap the benefits of your own sweetness--until that day no one else ever will.

Flowers of Friendship

For my Friend
who has been there for me
through thick and thin.
I just want you to know
that your friendship
is greatly appreciated.

Lots of love,
Your friend

Real Friendship

Real friendship
has nothing to be gained or lost.
It's just two people
accepting each other for who they are –
not who they want each other to be.
Real friends look for the good
in each other – not the bad.
Remember in order to HAVE a friend
you must first BE a friend.

Life...

My life and your life is a never-ending
journey of lessons to be learned –
sometimes happy and sometimes hurtful.
Many of us will "get" the lessons that make
life meaningful, but others will not.
They'll go on living confused, controlled and unfulfilled lives
without knowing why.

Are you "getting" your lessons?

Addictions

Any addiction will keep you from doing what's right;
in fact, some addictions will keep you up all night.
Stop trying to hide your problem
and face it head on.
This way your whole world doesn't get torn.
People see your world crumbling down around you.
They also see you running around
saying this but doing that.
Stop crying and saying that you can't make it.
Start praying to God and saying that
with His help you can make it...
Because you can and you will.
You Will, You Will, You Did.

Now, Live!

Are You a Victim of Yourself?

Do you feel as if everyone is in control of your life
but you're not?
You have the ability and control to change that.
Stop whining and complaining
about how miserable your life is.
Do something about it.
Change your thinking about yourself.
That's what has led you to this place in your life.
Stop people-pleasing and going along to get along.
Value yourself as a person worthy of respect – God does.
Don't always accept as truth what others say about
you. They have their own agenda for you.
Believe God when He says
you are fearfully and wonderfully made.
I challenge you to change the way you think
about yourself.
Change the way you allow others to treat you.
Accept the challenge -- you're worth it!
Take Control!

Stop Being a Victim of Yourself!

Be Yourself!

Be yourself, and you never have to play
the game of switch back.
You know what I mean.
Stop being what other people
want you to be, and just be you.
If they can't accept you,
you are in the wrong place.
I think that this is something
you don't want to face.
Give yourself a fair chance, and
be the best person that you can –
for you and for no one else.

You are worth it!

Being At Peace With Yourself

Love yourself
just as you would love another
for there are many times when
the rest of the world will be too busy
to care about you.
That will be the time you need to
call on the Lord and
be at peace with yourself.

Beware of the Liar and the Lie

A lie hurts all who are involved,
even the liar.
The liar is full of fear, false pride and
low self-esteem, justifying the lie.
The lie is made up of many things
except the truth!
In an effort to cover up lies
many bridges and relationships
are destroyed.
Remember this fact--
most liars can look you in your face
and lie very convincingly.

Take a Close Look!

Blessed!

You went to sleep last night without a care.
You woke up this morning without a dare.
How blessed you are!
Many people's lives are so filled
with tragedy and grief.
I still never see you pray.
The Lord loves you anyway.

You Are Blessed!

Chasing the Jeffersons

She's funny and very agreeable, as long as she can see
an opportunity to get a Jefferson or Grant.
She's your everything girl, go anywhere you want to.
She will do whatever you want to do.
She will neglect her family to get the Jefferson or Grant.
When the job is complete, she'll take her son to the mall.
She will by him a game or a gift to compensate for the abandonment
of her duties as a mother.
She rushes through the mall because she has to get back.
She'll stop at McDonald's on the way home because
she can't and has no time to cook.
Upon arrival from the store, she sits a moment in her place,
all the time thinking about what she has to do tonight.
It hurts her to be still; her thoughts are her enemy.
She once told me she buried her conscious a long time ago.
She must get the Jefferson or Grant.
She's never at home, just passes through.
Her children are raising themselves. They
have no respect for her at all.
They talk to her as if she was just another girl on the street.
She calls home every day to check on them
and tells them she loves them,
but does she?
Her true love is the Jefferson.
She'll cry at the drop of a dime; she appears to be very
compassionate but the tears are for herself.
They are the tears of resentment for having to live her life this way.
Sometimes it's men, sometimes it's women. She hates them all.
Most of all, she hates herself.
In the end, she gets the Jefferson, but no happiness.

Controlling Other People

You just can't do it!
But what you can do is pray to God
that He will take that unhealthy desire from you.
Think about yourself and ask yourself why
you must control others.
Truthfully speaking, who can we really control
besides ourselves?
People who can't or won't control themselves
are usually the ones who try to control others.
Let's be clear – I am not talking about children.
I'm speaking in reference to other grown folks.
People who try to control other people
lack something within themselves.
An empty hole inside you is waiting to be filled
with whomever or whatever,
but only God can fill it completely – ask Him!

Control Yourself and I Will Control Me!

Dirty Deeds

Be careful of what you do,
because all dirty deeds will return to you.
All of your deeds, good or bad,
will come back to you.
It is at that time you will ask yourself,
"Why is this happening to me?"
It will be revealed to you in your mind's eye,
and you will have your answer.
Ninety percent of the time this revelation
is never shared with anyone else.
While committing dirty deeds against others remember
you are hurting yourself, too.

Stop Doing Dirty Deeds!

Feeling Sorry

Who are you really feeling sorry for – me or you?
Does feeling sorry really help any situation or person?
Or does feeling sorry give you courage?
I used to think feeling sorry for someone helped them,
but I know better now.
I would much rather take those sorry feelings and turn them
them into positive power, enriched with enthusiasm and
guts to face whatever is coming.
We get caught up in feeling sorry
and miss the real point of what has happened,
therefore, we don't get the lesson and we don't grow.
Remember this, you can't live without learning.

Stop feeling sorry –
and LIVE!

Finding Your Passion

What makes your heart sing
and laces your soul with warmth?
Do you know?
So many people are out of touch with
what truly brings them joy.
I ask you, what is your passion?
Sometimes we lose our passion
because of relationships
we allow to enter our lives.
The drama and issues that other people bring
into our lives can sometimes take over our passion.
What I mean is, some friendships can be toxic.
We get so caught up with other people
that our passion slips away.

Set boundaries and allow no one to cross them.
This way, you can be a friend
and keep your Passion!

Live and Let Live!

A Good Life

Thank You, Lord, for waking me up this morning!
You are such a good God.
Even in times when I am undeserving,
You continue to love and bless me.
So many times in life we pray for the things
that are meaningless to our lives.
We want to feel good and not to think about
what we really do.
So often we put aside what's in our hearts
and what we know to be true.
We all want a **good life,**
but what are we willing to do to achieve this good life?
We wear masks of smiles until we are alone.
Then the mask falls from our faces
and the real is revealed.
A flood of sadness fills the face of the pretender.
Can't show who you really are; it's too painful
and why should you?
In your world all is fair weathered.

I Will Help You...If!

I will help you only if I can control your life.
I will help you if you take all my advice
and do as I say, not what I do.
Yes, I will help you to help myself.
That's who I'm really helping
to not think about how messed up my life is.
I will just control all of your situations.
This keeps my mind occupied.
I must come clean about my true motives;
the truth is that it hurts to think about my own life and situation.
It is easier to focus on other people
and give my opinions to them,
instead of facing the real problem.

I Need Help!

In Search Of The "Good Time"

In search of the "good time" much of life is missed,
many relationships are broken up, yes, many hearts
are broken – while looking for the "good time."

There are lots of little children who will never see their parents
just because of the "good time."
I have to get these shoes for this or that
outfit for the next "good time."
Bills go unpaid, responsibility is lacking
for the sake of the "good time."

Some people look as if they stepped out of a magazine,
but follow them home; you will need a bulldozer to get in.
Our integrity goes right down the drain
at the hand of the "good time."
We can't keep our word because we're in search of the
"good time."

Many people are on the run from life and are hiding
in the clubs and at parties.
They smile and laugh hard, but on the inside they are
crying and screaming for help and for love.
Yes, they want something that they themselves
are not capable of giving.
They want everyone around them to be responsible for
what they are lacking in themselves.

Many people are truly just living for the weekend –
in search of the "good time."

The M & M Story

This is a story not about candy—as a matter of fact there's
nothing sweet about this story at all. This story relates to
many, many women and their transition from young girl to
young woman. This transition is from *Mama to a Man.*

A young woman travels into adulthood, and she knows nothing about
what she's getting ready to experience. She leaves her mother's house,
feet never touching the ground, and lands right in her man's house.
She's afraid she won't be able to make a decent life on her own,
never looking inside and asking herself what does
she want to do with her life? She feels safer letting
someone else make her decisions for her.

She says she doesn't like someone making all her choices. I ask
why she went from her *Mama to her Man*, and she answers,
"Look at the fine car I drive, look at the big house I live in." I
ask, "But do these material things spell happiness for you?"
There is silence for a moment, and she looks at me and says
that she doesn't worry about a roof over her head or clothes on
her back and don't forget all the fine outfits that she wears.
I ask again, "But does all this equal happiness to you?"
She yells out that he's a good man, he works really hard.
Again, I can see she would really like to avoid this conversation;
no, not this time. We are going to get to the bottom of this one.
Her conversation is always him, always putting herself last.
I ask why again; she's getting angry with me, not really.
She's angry at herself for never stepping out on her own,
never sitting in the park and just admiring the beautiful flowers,
and watching the sun go down or watching the sun rise.

Yes, she is angry all right, but not with me. She knows all the things-
-the simple joys that make the heart smile—that she gave away.
She sacrificed who she really is

to people-please everyone except herself.

33

My Sista'

Let's walk in peace and love,
not envy and hate.
When you are down, talk to me.
I want to talk to you.
And when I am in despair,
I don't want to worry about you
spreading my business.
Let's be strong for each other and
keep each other prayed up!
Are you there for me?
Because I am there for you!

Sista' To Sista'

Pay Me My Money!!!

You came to me in desperation,
with nowhere else to turn.
You needed to borrow my money.
The only thing I ask you to do
is to pay me back!!
Just remember, the bridge you burn down
is the one you may need to cross again.

Pay Me My Money!!!

Permission

The world seems to be a nice place to be, then why are there
so many people committing suicide everyday. People are
just giving up on themselves and their ability to survive
in this world. I believe we give up when all we
have been our entire lives is a doormat, we eventually get tired of
being that. What we do with ourselves next is very important. Why
do we find it very hard to commit to change when it involves the most
important person to us. Yes I'm talking about YOU! We have not set
any boundaries so people walk all over our lives with our permission.
I know what you are saying, I did not give them permission, but
you see you really did, your silence gave them permission.

Real Happiness

Real happiness will only last temporarily
in the objects that we possess.
Real happiness comes from the pit of your soul and your heart.
Take a good look inside your life.
Are you really happy?
If not, know that you can be
by changing the direction of your life.

*It's all up to you
and God!*

Real Problem (Me)

At work you can always tell if she's seen her married boy friend this weekend or not. If she hasn't, look out world she'll be snapping and biting everyone's head off all week long. She's not living life; life is living her. She's angry at life because of the courage she lacks and refuses to tap into. She's quick to judge other people.

The weekends that she sees him, the following Monday she's very chipper and gay speaking to everyone "good morning and how are you doing." You can see the dismay on her co-workers' faces--as they walk away, they are laughing and saying, "She must have seen her boy friend this weekend." What's the real issue? It is such an obvious difference. She depends on her boy friend for all her happiness. She said he never buys her flowers, I ask why not plant your own garden.

She likes to give her opinion about everyone else's life and relationships. She never speaks of any personal situations in her life. Every waking hour she hates life until the moment he calls, and tells her exactly what she wants to hear. He knows just what to say to keep her going for now. She has put up with his excuses for the past twenty years. She's angry with the rest of the world, because she lacks the real courage to address her real problems, the problems at heart. She knows this man will never commit to her. Why does she keep holding on? But what is she holding on to? She's holding onto his promises, his lies. Why do his words lace her heart with such hope? Everyone around her can see she's being played the fool, why can't she see it? She knows what's happening-she's just living in a house of denial. Since the beginning of time society has taught us to paint a pretty picture, regardless of what the real problems are. It's easier for her to give it to the rest of the world, than to stand up and face the real problems in her life.

Self Love…

Does not allow abuse of any kind.
Don't kick my butt and then say
you love me, because you really don't.
Self Love tells me that I need
to remove myself and my things
into my own space and place.
That's where I will rebuild
my courage and respect for myself.

**Before I can really love another,
I must love myself!**

A Sista' Awareness Call

Sisters, we must stop looking for other sisters to feel superior to. I see sisters only accommodating themselves with other women that they feel are much less than themselves. We resent the thought of learning something from another sister. We make eye contact, but our lips remain sealed.

What's the real issue here? Is it your unsure feelings for me or does it lie within yourself? We are quick to roll our eyes and give a very unpleasant attitude. Again, where is this really coming from?

The social and economic levels of our lives may be different; however, we carry the same inner feelings. The difference is how we attempt to deal with situations – good or bad – which occur in our lives. That's a legitimate difference that separates us.

The fact that you wear your hair short and you're a size four, or she wears her hair braided and she's a vegetarian; these things do not define all that we are. These are only characteristic issues that define our tastes, what we like as opposed to dislike, that's all.

That doesn't mean that the quality of my life has a greater value than someone else's life. We breath the same air on the same God-given earth.

Let's all stop and think a moment. My life is only my life and your life is only your life. The events of my world are not your fault or your problem.

So let's not be judgmental of each other or make derogatory comments about one other. Whatever happened to greeting each other with a friendly smile and saying hello? This could have a tremendous impact on someone else's day.

As we begin to truly address our own negative forces in our lives and change them to positive ones, that's when we can expect our outlook on life to change.

Space Invaders

People call when their lives are upside down -- they need a loving and caring ear. They vent all the frustrations of their world; I mean they unload, THEY GIVE IT UP. When you hear from them something is always wrong. Has the phone ever rung and the caller on the other end begun a conversation with a simple hello, how was your day and then waited for an answer? I don't think so! Even close friends or people in our lives that claim to be close to us; they take from us and drain us emotionally of all that we have to give; they even steal your reserve if you let them. Everything is fine until the moment reverses itself. A change happens in the air, the universe. The minute you need them everybody disappears, vanishes. You find yourself all alone, like you truly are -- ALL ALONE -- Until the next time they need you.

People enter our lives for so many reasons; they take what they need to maintain balance and stability in their lives, and then ther're gone, to deal as best they can with the world they know. We live in a world of emotionally crippled individuals constantly seeking crutches to lean on and support them. I can't remember the last time someone called and simply said thanks for always being there for me. I can't remember the last time someone simply said thank you for easing my pain. All the kindness we give out makes me wonder -- will any of it ever make its way back to us?

Stand Up!

Pray that you can stand up and deliver
for yourself.
Trust that you will be guided
in the right direction for your life.
Follow **your** dreams, not someone else's,
so that you don't end up
with a heart full of regrets.
Praise the good in yourself and others.
Never forget that it could always be
the other way!
Don't ask what way; you know what way.

There's Only One Way!

The Sideline of Your Life

You're standing on the sideline
watching everything happen to you and around you.
You say: he does this to me and she did that to me;
things just keep happening to me;
a lot of bad things are all around me.

Now I ask you, why are you allowing
all these negative forces into your life?
Get off the sideline of your life and get into the game –
your game!

Get some new plays for yourself.
Stop playing what others want you to play.
It's on you now to make a move that you can live with.
Just do something beside standing and
watching your entire life pass before you.
Some people remain on the sideline for an entire lifetime,
complaining constantly about their lives and
never doing anything about it.
I am coming to you as a friend because
I really do care about you.

Now Step Out and Live!!

What's In Your Cup?

Are you happy with what's in your cup?
If not, try something different and new.
Stop settling for what
you have right now.
Pour out what's in your cup
and fill it with something
you've always wanted to do.
All you need is some faith in God
and a little courage--
you'll be just fine.

Now Drink Up!

When All You Have is Alcohol

You are living inside of the bottle;
Constantly on the run from yourself.
There is something going on inside of you
that you refuse to address.
One day you will have to look at it
and get a handle on it
or it will handle you.

Please Get Help for Yourself!

Who Am I?

I live the life that my parents want me to.
The pressure is so great,
my insides are constantly turning around.
I must make my family happy,
but what about me?
What about who I really am?
What about my true feelings?
I can't love who I really love.
I can't really love.
I am sick a lot.
Who am I?
I am who my family needs me to be.
I can't be who I really am -
it makes my family look bad.

But, who am I?

Wing of Kindness

You are the kind of person
that would help anyone if you could.
Nice, without a hidden agenda,
just an opportunity to help.
Your kindness is rare and pure.
You carry many on your
wing of kindness,
Most of all…

Thanks for Helping Me!

Words Hurt

Be careful not to say things
that will damage a relationship forever.
Friends or lovers or family
– it doesn't matter –
A harsh word can't be erased.
Be slow to lash out in anger.
Once you've really thought about it,
you'll see
it just wasn't worth it anyway.
Stop hurting each other.

You Can Make It!

You can make it even if you can't see your
hands in front of your face right now.
You can make it!
When friends are few and
when bad luck is your only luck
You can still make it!
Know in your heart that
you are worth the struggle and
keep moving straight ahead.

You Can Make It!

You Go Girl!

You are truly a woman of substance.
I see you doing what's best for your life
and doing a great job at it.
Your kind heart overwhelms everyone around you.
You really got it goin' on.
You don't live by the Joneses.
You have set your own course in life.
Mr. Goodbar is only a candy bar in your life.
You don't use and you don't get used.
Love is all around you because
you are the love that you give.
The Lord is very important to you.
God loves you and so do I.

You Go Girl!

Your Life!

Your life is not a stage play or an act
for people to sit and enjoy.
When the curtains fall,
there will be no Act II.
I want you to realize that every new day you
experience is a gift from God,
not another scene in a play.
Take a serious look at your life and get on the right track – His track.
I know you can do it – He's waiting for you to come to Him.

I am praying for you!

Your Smile...

Is warm and inviting.
It welcomes me and invites me
to stay awhile and cherish the moment.
You ask for nothing, and yet you give everything
in the warmth of your smile.
You make everyone you meet
want to do a little more
as they enter your door.
A wealthy spirit you are,
rich with compassion and kindness.
Your smile is a wonderful place to visit.
I truly appreciate your smile.

See Ya Soon!

Your Word

Is your word any good?
Think about your answer.
The last time you obligated yourself
did you keep your word?
It is very important to yourself and others that you keep your word.
What comes out of your mouth tells the world what you are all about.

Keep your Word!

Love...

We can't always guard our hearts from the
pain that comes with loving others,
but at some point in our lives, the head will have to rule the heart.

Who's ruling yours?

My Dream

At the very first sight of your face a warm feeling laced my entire body. My thoughts left me without permission. I was lost for a second; left with a smile that I wore only for you. You smiled back and at that very moment, and I mean that very moment, you and I were in the room alone.

We talked about our childhood dreams, and what we wanted for ourselves when we grew up. Some dreams had come true and others just faded away.

Each time you smiled this feeling went through my body. I noticed that you talk with your hands. Every time you touched me by accident I lost focus on what you were saying. I said to my best friend once that I did not believe there was a Love out there for me. I guess I did as a lot of people do, looked for Love in the wrong places and things.

Sometimes the Love we crave is not the best Love for us, and we know this already. We have these talks with ourselves, and what do we do when it's time to stand and deliver? Our good common sense takes a back seat as we wear matters of the heart on our sleeve like a fly just waiting to jump into the wind.

Everything I have been searching for fell at my feet the moment I set eyes on you. I realize you came here with someone else, and it's not right of me to monopolize all of your time, but I do it anyway; what the hell, I may never see you again.

Loving You

Loving you is just like breathing. Yes, it's that easy.
I think of your smile, and my mind and body become light as
a feather. I don't have to think to love you, I just do.
The world appears to be a much better place to live when
loving you. I know, because loving you has enhanced my
perception and understanding of my world.
Don't misunderstand -- I don't mean to sound incomplete or
inadequate; I am one with God first. I have been blessed with
your love and kindness to no end. In the world we live in,
real love is a rare jewel. You are just that -- something wonderful.
I can sit in a room filled with people and
just watch you and your movement and become overwhelmed
to the point of embarrassment. I sweat in the palms of my
hands and my heart skips a beat at the very thought of you.
I try to look at you without you noticing me, but you catch me
every time and we both blush. Life itself is much
more wonderful in love. People search away most of their lives
looking for love in all the wrong places and people. We try
to make love, reform love, invent love, create love. STOP!
Love is, as it will always be. If love is meant to be, it will be –
just as loving you is easy for me.

Still loving you,

Me

The Power of Love...

Can make you soar
to the height of an eagle.
Nothing is too hard with the power
of love in your life.
Love is courage with a smile.
Love is fuel to one's heart.

Keep Loving Me!

Love Sounds

We are in perfect harmony
with each other; when you're high
and I'm low, how perfect we flow.
The beats you deliver
make my inside shiver.
The music of love is ever flowing
and that's the love "thang"
that keeps me glowing.
The music that we make
is nothing more than
the love we give and take.
The Sweet Sounds of Love

At Love's End

I thought we would be together forever.
In the beginning we could not stay apart too long.
Calling each other during the day,
making plans to spend time together.
Wherever you were, that's where I wanted to be.
Most of my thoughts were about you, loving you,
sitting next to you, holding hands.
What happened to the closeness we shared?
Now you're in one room and I'm in another.
What happened to the love?
I saw it coming, but I didn't see it leave.
How could I have missed it?
Maybe it left when I was with my friends and
you were with yours.
Maybe it left when I was waiting
for your phone call that I never got.
I think it may also have left
while I sat at the dinner table alone
wondering where you were.
The end of love is not a friendly place to be.
I asked myself the famous question, "What did I do?"
knowing the answer in my head and in my heart.
Even though I know that this is the end of love
and what is best for me,
I can't convince my heart of this fact.
I know that before I can start anew, the old must end.
I am now ready to move forward with my life
and my love.

Movin' On!

It is time for me to move on with my life.
We tried to have something
that was not designed for you or me together.
Maybe a friendship will be possible
later on down the road,
but for now, I must move on.
The lies I caught you in hurt,
and you still tried to hide your dirt.
I must move on!
I know I must walk through a painful forest
to see the beautiful rainbow.
I have the courage because I know of another
place where I will shine and smile again.
The journey I will make now will be about me not we!
I will cleanse myself of the pain, anger, and lies
and move on to a place of light and new ground.
Thanks for the lesson -- you taught me well.

For today, I shall move on.

One Love

We are using the wrong math
in our relationships.
When two people come together
to share their lives,
1+1 does not equal 2! 1+1=1.
In a relationship
two whole and complete people
come together to make
a whole and complete union.
Each person must be loving,
supportive, respectful, and generous
to their individual selves
before they can offer more of the same
to their partner.

All That I Have I Give To You!

63

Religion...

Religion is not the talk you talk or the place you go to worship –
it's how you live your life each day
in a close, personal RELATIONSHIP with Jesus Christ.
Talk to HIM, then listen!

Talk to the Lord!

Tell Him all about your problems.
Open your heart, ask for help
and then let it go.
Let the Lord do His will
in your life.
He knows all about you and
every situation in your life.

Talk to the Lord!

About The Author

Chantay D. Mahogany is a motivational speaker, poet, support group leader, founder and president of The StoryTime Network, Inc. For the past eight years she has facilitated workshops for half-way houses and homeless shelters for women, teaching them life skills and self-esteem through speaking, writing and interactive exercises.

The idea for helping women came to her while she was employed as a Washington, D.C. Corrections Officer. She realized that her unit was filled with repeat offenders and wondered why. One day, she decided to ask a senior repeat offender, who was nearly 60 years old, why it was that she kept returning to prison. The inmate stared at her for a moment and then said, "When this lifestyle is all you know, this is all you can do." Ms. Mahogany replied, "Has anyone ever told you that you can change what you know and what you do?" The inmate just stared at her and walked away.

It was at that moment that Ms. Mahogany discovered her life's mission – to help women see that they CAN make choices to change direction, to rebuild their lives and continue their journey on the good paths. After all...she did it!

Printed in the United States
50782LVS00007B/217-333